1, 2: Judo-Karate. 3: Field Hockey. 4: Fencing.

1

5-9: Baseball.

10, 13, 14: Baseball. 11: Softball. 12: Cricket.

15

16

17

18

19

15–18: Basketball. 19: Boxing.

20-23: Football. 24: Handball.

25-29: Golf.

30, 32: Diving. 31, 33: Swimming. 34: Water Polo.

35

36

37

38

39

35-39: Tennis.

8

40

41

42

40, 41: Ice Hockey. 42: Tennis.

43: Lacrosse. 44: Gymnastics.
45: Rugby. 46: Polo. 47, 48: Soccer.

49

50

51

52

49-52: Gymnastics.

53-60: Running.

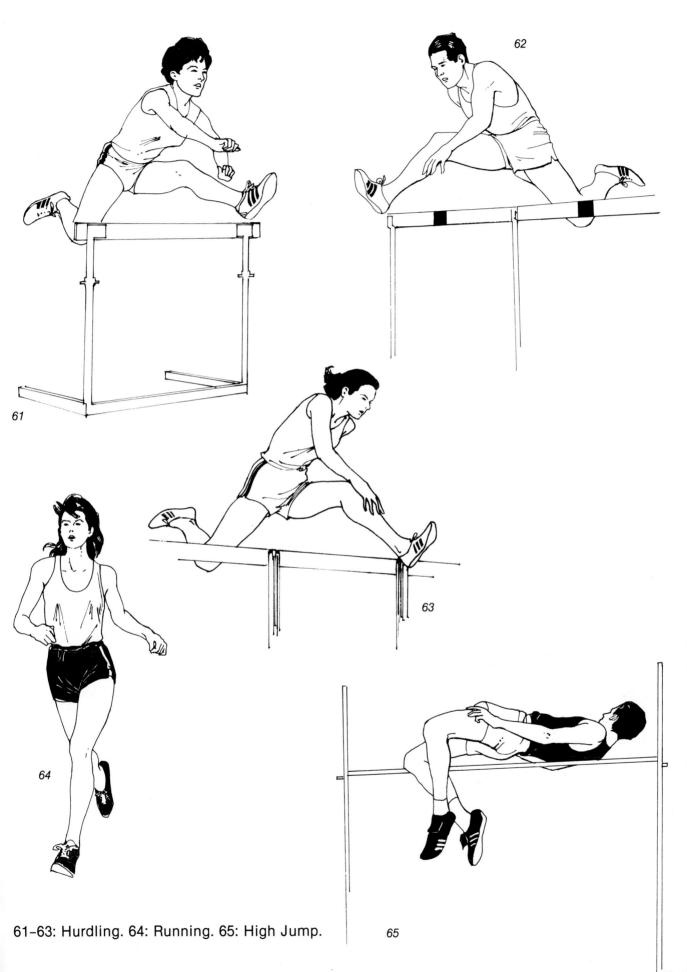

61–63: Hurdling. 64: Running. 65: High Jump.

66, 67: Pole Vault. 68, 69: Long Jump. 70: Discus Throw.

71, 72: Relay Running. 73, 74: Discus Throw.

75, 76: Volleyball. 77: Squash. 78: Shot Put.

79, 80: Javelin Throw. 81–83: Shot Put.

84: Weightlifting. 85: Freestyle Wrestling. 86: Walking.
87: Equestrian Competition.

88, 90: Rodeo. 89: Badminton.

88

89

90

91

91: Yacht Racing.

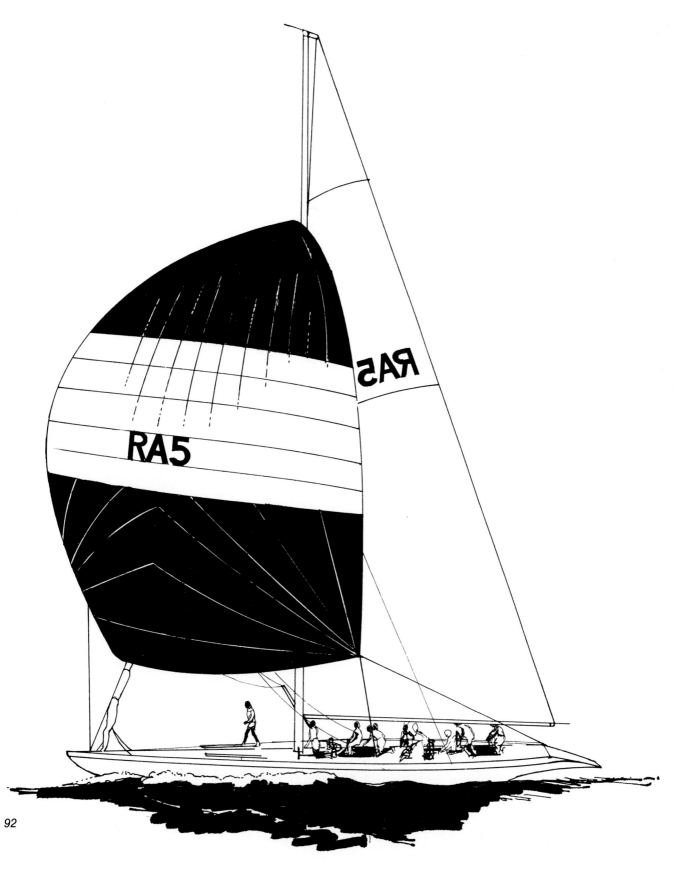

92

92: Yacht Racing.

93

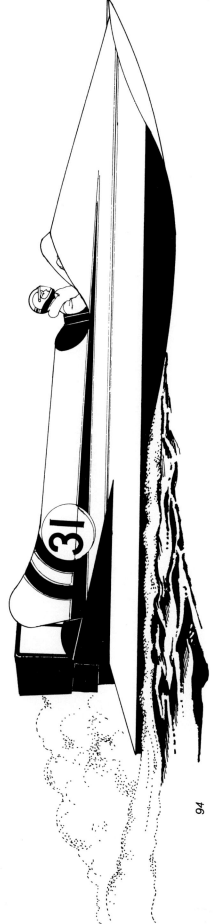

94

93, 94: Powerboat Racing.

95

96

95, 96: Rowing.

97

98

99

100

99: Paddle Tennis. 100: Drag Racing.

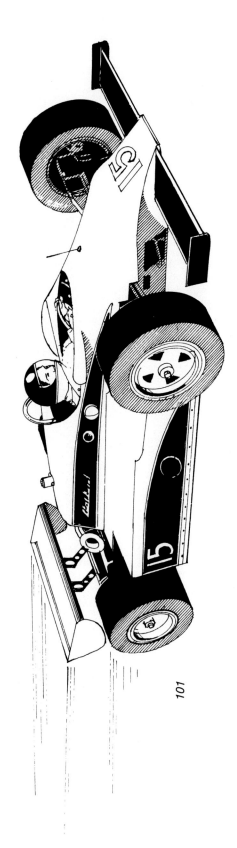

101

102

101: Indianapolis-type Racing. 102: Formula 1 "Grand Prix" Racing

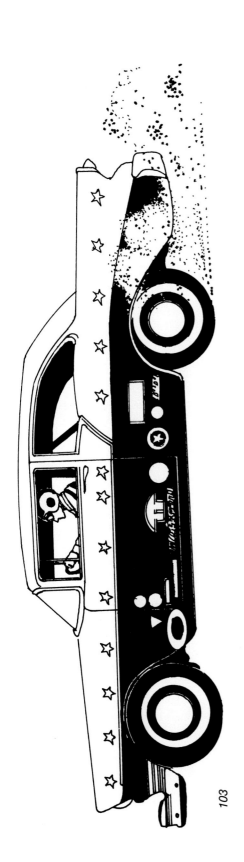

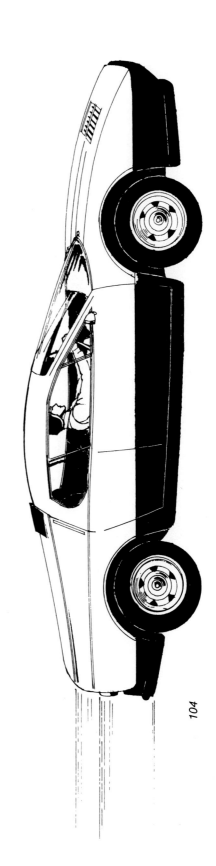

103: Stock Car Racing. 104: Sports Car Racing.

105

106

107

108

105–108: Automobile Racing.

109

110

109: Ski Jumping. 110, 111: Skiing.

111

112

113

114

112–114: Figure Skating. 115: Bicycle Racing.

115

116: Bobsledding. 117, 119, 120: Speed
Skating. 118: Motorcycle Racing.

INDEX

3 5758